WALKING

in

FAITH

Testimony and Teaching

By
Tim Greenwood

You may contact the author at:

Tim Greenwood Ministries
P. O. Box 1904
Arcadia, CA 91077

Walking in Faith

ISBN 0-9666-6890-1
Copyright ©1998 Tim Greenwood

Published by:

𝔇eclaration 𝔓ublishers
www.declarationpublishers.com

Revision No. 20080820

Contents

Chapter 1
First Things First

God is love:
(1 John 4:16) And we have known and believed the love that God hath to us. God is love; and he that dwells in love dwells in God, and God in him.

God is full of compassion and mercy:
(Psa. 86:15) But thou, O Lord, art a God full of compassion, and gracious, longsuffering, and plenteous in mercy and truth.

God is no respecter of persons:
(Acts 10:34) Then Peter opened his mouth, and said, of a truth I perceive that God is no respecter of persons.

God does *ONLY* good!
(Prov. 11:23) The desire of the righteous is only good: but the expectation of the wicked is wrath.
(Luke 18:19) And Jesus said unto him, Why callest thou me good? None is good, save one, that is, God.

*God **DID NOT** put sickness on you!* ***It IS God's will to heal...*** *YOU!* Every good and perfect gift comes from the Father. It *IS* God's will to heal you.

How do I know?

I know because His Word, the Bible, says so. Now, you just need to believe, (have faith in), what He has *ALREADY* said, in that Word. And *LEARN* to receive the good things He has for you, ***including*** your healing.

4

Chapter 2
What About Healing?

When I first attended services in a church that practiced healing the sick, back in the late 60's, I heard a sermon on the subject of healing and anointing with oil. I sat through this sermon with a migraine headache, one of the many over the previous few months. After services, I thought I would *try it out* and be anointed. Immediately the migraine went away, and I am happy to say that I have *NEVER* had another one since. I was healed.

I had been prayed for and anointed with oil many times since, for this and that, (never anything really serious). Sometimes I received healing, and sometimes I did not.

It seemed to me that the more mature I became as a Christian, the less often I received healing.

I found this to be somewhat confusing.

Was it God? Was it me? Had I lost my initial zeal?
I did not know the answer.

Note: **At age 45, I found myself being rushed into open-heart surgery. I recovered quickly and began to return to normal life, only to be rushed back into the hospital. There, after dozens of tests, the doctors came in and gave me the bad news. They said that the surgery had failed, and that I was going to die, and that there was nothing more they could do for me. All they could offer was a heart transplant, which I declined. They sent me home to die.**

Through this experience, I have had to heavily focus on the subjects of **faith and healing**.

I came to understand that sometimes God *WOULD* heal us on the faith of *ANOTHER PERSON*. (This is how I had been healed on all previous occasions.) I believe that this is so that we can *SEE* that healing by faith really *WORKS!*

At this time, I really did not understand that there was any benefit to having my own faith because I had always depended on the minister's faith and on the faith of other people that would include my situations in their prayers.

But now, for the first time in my life, the situation was truly desperate. In retrospect, at this point I was spiritually dead and had no hope or faith of my own.

So, I went on a campaign and began to request prayers.

At one point, I had massed nearly 1000 wonderful people, from my denomination and from many others. I had hands laid on me, and was anointed with oil four or five times based on my desire to be healed, the faith of the minister, the prayers and faith of all these people, and my faith that God can and does, sometimes, heal people.

It seems however, that God will only heal on another's faith a number of times, just to get us started, (*when we are still baby Christians*). After this, (*when we **should** be matured*), it seems that God expects us to begin to exercise *OUR OWN FAITH*. This is why sometimes, I did not receive healing. I *KNEW* that God could heal. I knew that He does heal.

In retrospect, I did not understand *anything* about faith. I, like so many others, just thought I did. Then I began learning some things about faith.

Chapter 3
What About Faith?

(Mat. 17:20) [*Jesus speaking:*] ... **verily,** [*I'm telling you the truth, when*] **I say unto you** [*YOU!*]**, If ye** [*YOU!*] **have faith as** [*little as*] **a grain of mustard seed** [*about the size of the head of a straight pin*]**, ye** [*YOU!*] **shall say unto this mountain, remove hence to yonder place** [*I command you to get out of my path!*]**; and it shall remove** [*then the mountain will get out of my path!*]**; and nothing** [*NOTHING!*] **shall be impossible unto YOU.**

How many of you have tried *this* scripture out on one your local hills or mountains, telling it to move ... to no avail?

I always thought this scripture to be a little odd, with Jesus seemingly rubbing our noses in just how little faith we have. But I came to find out, that is not the case at all!

The focus is *NOT* on how little faith we have, but rather on *FAITH itself*, and how to put it to work for us!
So, that brings up several questions:

Why did your hill or mountain, not move?
This type of thing can and has caused many to question what they call their "faith."

Is my faith my religious affiliation or denomination?
That can't be right, because Jesus said that we were supposed to have some *quantity* of faith, and an *affiliation* would be *a* faith.

Is my faith my personal set of beliefs?
That can't be right for the same reason.

Is my faith just my belief in a Supreme Being and that Jesus is His Son? That can't be right either, because that would mean that we either have faith or we don't have faith. And, *Rom. 12:3* says that we have been given "the measure of faith."

Is my faith, that God or Jesus can or will do something? That can't be right either!

So then: What is faith?
Where does faith come from?
How do we get it?
How do we know if we already have *ANY* faith?
How do I use this faith?

Read on for the answers.

Chapter 4
What Is Faith?

(Heb. 11:1) Faith is the substance of things hoped for, **the evidence of things not seen.**

Where does faith come from?
(Rom. 10:17) **Faith comes by hearing,** and hearing by **the Word of God.**

Do we have *ANY* faith?
(Rom. 12:3) For I say, ... **to every man that is among you,** ... to think soberly, **according as God hath dealt to every man the measure of faith.**

If we believe the Word of God and have accepted the sacrifice of Jesus Christ and are reading and hearing that Word, then we *DO HAVE at least* the faith of a mustard seed!

Yes, even if our measure of faith is tiny, *we do have enough!* So then, why does the mountain *not move?* Because, this scripture is an analogy... a *very important* analogy. I had been going to church and a student of the Bible for over 25 years before I understood this.

What a revelation to realize that *this mountain is analogous and symbolic of whatever seemingly huge, immovable problem, (or even some terrible illness), that is blocking our way in life.* And, this wonderful scripture tells us *exactly* what to do.

We are to step up and face this mountainous problem, and *SAY* to it *"GET out of my way... and GO jump in the lake!"* Like casting out a demon, in the power and name of Jesus.

9

(Mark 11:23) "For verily I say unto you, That *whosoever* shall **SAY** unto this mountain, be thou removed, and be thou cast into the sea; and *shall not doubt in his heart, but shall* **BELIEVE** that those things, which he *SAITH,* shall come to pass; he shall have *whatsoever* he **SAITH**.

(Mark 11:24) "Therefore I say unto you, *What things so ever* ye desire, when ye pray, **BELIEVE that ye receive them, and ye shall have them.**"

Have what? You shall have whatever you **SAID!**

Faith, is not your "religion."
Faith, is not just a state of mind.
Faith is more than believing *IN* God and Jesus.
Faith is more than belief that God or Jesus *can* or even *will* do something!

Faith is the **BELIEVING** that we **ALREADY HAVE**, what we **SAID** we were asking for. (And the SAYING is just as important as the BELIEVING). Faith is belief that God has **ALREADY** done something *because His Word said He would!* Because, faith is *BELIEVING* and trusting God, and then *ACTING* on that belief and trust.

So, real Bible faith is believing what the Word of God says, so much, that you step out and *ACT* upon it.

When I learned this, I immediately got a degree better, but still kept experiencing some of the symptoms. I was sure that I was still missing something, so I kept looking until I found the answers.

You see, faith is not just something that you have. It is something that you have to use! James 2:14-26 says that faith without corresponding actions is dead!

Chapter 5
You vs. The Devil

Jesus stripped, (spoiled or disarmed), the devil and his de mons of all their weapons, their entire armor, all their power and authority and then humiliated all of them!

(Col. 2:14) ... Blotting out the handwriting of ordinances that was against us, which was contrary to us, and took it out of the way, nailing it to His cross.

(Col. 2:15) And **having spoiled principalities and powers, He [Jesus] made a show of them openly, triumphing over them in it.**

And Jesus even took the devil's keys!

(Rev. 1:18) I am He that liveth, and was dead; and behold, I am alive for evermore, Amen; and [I, Jesus,] **have the keys of hell and of death.**

On the other hand, Jesus has given *us* the authority to use *His Name* in authority over all things.

He gave us a legal Power of Attorney, to use His name to do all that He did and more! And that Name. *The Name of JESUS is above ALL other names in Heaven and Earth!*

(Eph. 1:21) **Far above** all principality, and power, and might, and dominion, and **every name that is named**, not only in this world, but also in that which is to come.

(Phil. 2:9) Wherefore God also hath highly exalted Him, and given Him **a name, which is above every name**.

11

Note: Christ is *NOT* Jesus' last name. (But that is another subject that you can read about on the TGM website at **www.tgm.org**.) Just remember that **Jesus *IS*** the name.

ALL other names must bow, (i.e., submit), to the NAME of JESUS.

(Remember: ***Everything has a name.*** (i.e.) Satan is a name; depression is a name; diabetes is a name; heart disease is a name; cancer is a name.)

His *name, **JESUS***, has power! This authority gives our words power.

God created mankind and gave him dominion and authority in the earth. Adam, that first man, committed high treason by handing over that dominion to Satan.

Satan held dominion and power in the earth *until* JESUS defeated him and took possession of that dominion and authority.

Then, before He ascended into Heaven, JESUS *gave us* that dominion and authority through the use of His name. There will be more on this later on in the book.

The devil *no longer* has any power or authority of his own. It's only a bluff, like a bully on the school yard.

He has to use ***YOUR*** own authority against ***YOU*** and he does this by using ***YOUR*** own negative words.

If you *refuse* to allow the devil to talk you out of your healing, then there isn't any way that he can keep you from being healed.

12

Chapter 6
Stand On The Word

God sent His Word to heal you, (Psa. 107:20), and His Word works! He keeps His Word. So (this is important), *don't let lingering symptoms discourage you.* Your healing may be instantaneous, but if not, don't let doubts arise just because you do not see immediate results. It may take time for you to feel completely healed. So what do you do in the mean time?

1. God's Word is the final authority.
The Word says that *by His stripes you were healed!* (1Peter 2:24, past tense), quoted from (Isa. 53:4-5, future tense). Receive your healing as *already* taken place.

2. Refuse doubt and unbelief.
When the devil attacks you and makes you think you're still having *symptoms*, or whispers *words of doubt and unbelief* into your mind, deal with it immediately. Cast them down, rebuke and bind them, in Jesus name, (Mat. 16:19, 18:18). *And praise God for your healing!* The Greek word for "rebuke" means "to superimpose a value upon." So when you rebuke, you must set its value compared to the value of the Word of God and verbablly put what you are rebuking in its place.

Don't dwell on the symptoms; don't accept the devil's arguments, deception and lies. *Anything* that is a stumbling block to your faith, *is darkness and of the devil.* They may come through your own body and mind, family, friends, doctors or even your well-meaning pastor. I do not care *where* you hear or see stumbling blocks, do not accept them. (Rom. 14:1) Receive him that is weak in the faith, but *NOT* to doubtful disputations.

3. Refuse to believe everything you see and feel.
If what you see or feel contradicts the Word, only believe the Word. What you see and feel is not always real, but may be

13

manifestations of the devil to cause fear, doubt and unbelief. I know this first-hand! This is where many lose the battle!

4. Meditate On God's Word.

Concentrate on the Word, not on the illness. Meditation is the antidote to worry. Immerse yourself in the Word, reading out loud, particularly the healing scriptures. Even listen to audios of the Word as much as possible. ("Receive Your Healing Now!" on 2 CDs. Available from the TGM online catalog: **www.tgm.org**.)

Do you need faith? Faith comes from hearing the Word of God. Fill yourself through the eyes and ears with the Word of God until it fills you up, and overflows out of your mouth. This will release faith, and faith releases grace and healing. (Luke 6:45) ...for out of the abundance of the heart, the mouth speaks.

5. Do Not Fear!

What did Jesus repeatedly say? "Fear not!"... "Do not fear!" (Luke 8:50). What do the angels say every time they appear? "Fear not!" God will place a hedge about you. *But,* fear is a gateway in that hedge, which allows the devil to get to you. This is because *fear* is the devil's counterfeit of faith and is part of darkness. Light, (faith), cannot coexist with darkness, (fear). The devil will use every trick, lie, and deception, to cause you to fear and to open the gate. He is ever watchful of that gate. Therefore, keep it closed and locked by consistently renewing and increasing your faith.
(Rom. 8:15) ...you have not received the *spirit of bondage,* again to *fear*... ; (1 John 4:18) ...perfect *love casts out* fear....

6. Praise God For Your Healing.

How would you praise and thank God if you knew that you were healed this instant? Then praise Him like that *NOW*! Praising God for your healing, before you see a manifestation, is the highest form of faith. (This *IS* the shield of faith!) And afterwards, thank God *every day* that you are healed.

14

7. Do Not Waiver!

(James 1:6) James said that the person who waivers in his faith should not expect to receive *anything* from the Lord. (1 Tim. 6:12) ...fight the good fight of faith....

(Eph. 6:12) ...For we wrestle not against flesh and blood, but against principalities, powers, rulers of darkness and spiritual wickedness.

(Eph. 6:13) Therefore put on **the *whole* armor of God** and stand your ground. And having done all to stand... *STAND*!

In this context: Salvation, Righteousness, Truth and the preparation of the Gospel will provide you with protection. The Word of God, (*"It is written: ..."*), is to offensively rebuke the devil, (your sword). And faith, is to defend against the manifestations of the devil. Once the manifestation has been rebuked, and then it *seems* to return, begin to praise God. (Father, I praise You and thank You that I no longer have to believe what I see or feel.)

This kind of praise is your defense, (your shield), and has proven to be even more effective against darkness than using your sword.

8. Speak Only The Positive!

Speak only words that are in agreement with God's will for your healing. You have to *BELIEVE* you are healed, and that is impossible if you are constantly talking about *your* sickness. (If Jesus bore *your* sickness, then *your* sickness is gone! What is on you now, *does not belong to you! Therefore, do not lay claim to it.* Remember, your words have power to do both good and evil. The devil *will use your negative words* against you! That sickness belongs to the devil.)

Therefore, every day, let *God, the devil,* and *your body* know, by what you *SAY*, that you *believe* that you *have received* your healing, (Mark 11:23-24).

15

What you *SAY* is important!
(Mat. 12:36) In the day of judgment, men shall give account of *EVERY* idle word they have spoken!

If you are not sure how to pray for healing, you might recite or pray something like the following:

"Heavenly Father,
I thank You for Your Word that says that by the stripes of Jesus I am healed. I choose to believe that Your healing power went to work in my body the very instant that I believed Your Word.

Jesus Christ is Lord over my life - spirit, soul and body. I have received the power of God to make me sound, whole, delivered, saved and healed.

Sickness, disease, pain,
I resist you in the Name of Jesus. You are not the will of God.
I enforce the Word of God on you. I will not tolerate you in my life.
My days of sickness and disease are over!
Jesus bore my sickness, weakness and pain, and I am forever free!

Father,
Thank You for watching over Your Word to perform it on my behalf. I thank You and praise You in the mighty Name of Jesus!" Amen

This kind of prayer proclaims, (says), to God, the devil and everyone else, that you believe that the Word of God is true, and that the Word says that you are healed!

Chapter 7
The Healing Scriptures

The following scriptures are promises you can stand on to receive your healing:

Exodus 15:26	**Exodus 23:25-26**
Psalm 103:1-5	**Psalm 107:19-20**
Proverbs 4:20-23	**Isaiah 53:4-5**
Jeremiah 1:12	**Jeremiah 30:17**
Matthew 8:17	**Matthew 15:30-31**
Matthew 18:18-19	**Mark 11:23-24**
Mark 16:17-18	**Luke 9:2**
Luke 13:16	**Acts 5:16**
Acts 10:38	**Galatians 3:13-14**
James 4:7	**James 5:14-15**

These scriptures are all on the TGM website: **www.tgm.org**.

Take your Bible or go to the web site and read each of the above scriptures, *out loud.* That's right, I said, *out loud!* Read them loud enough, so that you can hear them with your own ears.

How would it make you feel, if God Himself spoke to you, like He did to Noah, and said, *"You are my child, and I LOVE you!"*

Please understand that this *IS* God, speaking ... to *YOU*, through the written record of what He has already said! Meditate on each phrase, and feel God's care, compassion and love, in His Word. Receive His Word as Him speaking to you. *And, apply His Word to your situation.*

Chapter 8
Putting It All To Work

As part of the process of learning all of this, there came the time that I had to act on my faith in God's Word. I had to start doing what I could not otherwise do, due to the sickness. For me, this involved walking more than 20 feet. So, with Marcia's help, I made my way out to the sidewalk to begin.

Now, manifestations of symptoms of heart disease vary from person to person, but the main symptom, angina, for me manifested as follows. I would feel tightness in my left chest, which would spread up and along the collarbone, under the arm causing a spreading "charley-horse" behind the left shoulder.

This would magnify and cause "charley-horses" on both sides of my neck and in the left upper arm. The pain would continue to intensify until I could feel my feet begin balling up into fists. Tears ran down my face, my lower teeth ached and the pain felt like a fire just above the left elbow and just behind the left shoulder. My heart was pounding out of my chest, I could not catch even a partial breath and I became light-headed and sick to my stomach as I felt all the blood draining from my face.

It would hold like this for a few moments and then all would subside, leaving me totally drained and gasping for air. Once they began, unless I would immediately sit down, regulate my breathing and heart rate, the attacks would fully manifest as described.

We began walking. At about 20 feet, an attack began. I told Marcia and we both began rebuking sickness, disease and the devil. By the time we said, "in the name of Jesus" the attack had already spread under my arm, but instantly stopped in its tracks! We walked about another 20 feet. Another attack manifested, was rebuked and also stopped, (this time before it got to my underarm). This process continued, never varying, with attacks occurring every 20 feet.

18

By the end of the fourth day, I was really frustrated, *VERY* angry at the devil, and so sore from the accumulated starts of attacks that my torso was leaning to the left.

When we got about three fourths the way around the block, I couldn't take it anymore! I threw a fit holding up my hands and face to God and screaming, "God, *how long* do I have to *ENDURE* this!?"

(I had thought that if I just kept doing this long enough, then God would just heal me. After venting my frustration, I asked God to forgive me, and told Him that I knew that He wasn't withholding anything from me.)

I then knew in my heart that I was still missing something. And that night I found it. I found that on my walks I had been successfully using the *Sword of the Spirit of the Word*, rebuking the devil based on scripture, similar to Jesus' example on the mount of temptation. (i.e) "It is written ..."

With the leading of the Holy Spirit, I realized that what I had been missing was the *Shield of Faith* spoken of in Ephesians 6. And that I needed to re-read Mark 11:22-24 as the framework of using my faith. While reading it, the Holy Spirit asked, "How would you express to God, that you truely do "believe and doubt not" that you receive what you said?" And before I could answer, He said "*PRAISE HIM* for it!" "Yes, even *BEFORE* it manifests in the natural!"

Part of me could not wait to get out to the sidewalk and try this out! But, another part did not want to chance another full-blown attack that may come if I was wrong. I decided then and there, this was literally, going to be *do or die*. I had made up my mind that I was *NOT,* going to be defeated by the devil.

The next morning, we began walking. At 20 feet, the attack came, was rebuked and stopped. At 20 more feet another attack began. This time I used the Shield of Faith and said,

"Father God, we have rebuked the spirit of sickness and disease, and I praise You and thank You for Your Word that says ...

He was wounded for our transgressions, He was bruised for our iniquities: the chastisement of our peace was upon Him; and with His stripes we were, and are, healed.

I believe Your Word, MORE than I believe ANY manifestation of sickness that the devil can place in me, MORE than I believe the reality of the material world!"

The attack stopped as it had before, but there was a difference...

We got 20 more feet, and this time *no attack* came and I was able to walk 40 feet! Double what I could before. But at 40 feet another attack began to manifest.

We immediately praised God like before using the Shield of Faith and the attack stopped, and on we walked, this time 80 feet, again *doubling* the distance! Then, *DOUBLE* that and **DOUBLE** that... and, it's been like that ever since.

Now, I am praising God nearly all the time.

I think I have become an actual, **Praise Addict**! And may I *never* be delivered from that.

God is so GOOD!

Chapter 9
Conclusions

WARNING!! I feel that you need to be warned, or forearmed, about something. Satan is happy just to keep you *in a state of Non-Resistance*. But should you disturb that status-quo, (say by acting on your faith and winning a victory over his influence), he will likely come against you in some way to attempt to negate that victory. If you are too strong, then he may come at you from another direction or through someone close to you. Therefore... while you are celebrating your victory, keep your armor on, your sword and your shield at the ready and be on guard!

IMPORTANT:

What you have just been taught is *NOT* just something that you use when you get sick. Once you start this, you *CANNOT* quit. It *MUST* become a *Way of Life*! You must get in line with God's Word, make changes in your life and develop your fellowship with Him. If you don't, you run the risk of loosing your healing during a counter-attack.

You see, even the greatest of sinners can receive the miracle of healing. However, continued Divine Health requires receiving Jesus as your Lord and Savior and obedience to and trust in God's Word. And you need to do this based upon your intimate knowledge of God's love for you. Knowing that God loves you so much that He will do what He said that He would do.

This is really all you need. I could have written volumes on this very deep and rich subject, but this basic teaching is all you really need to receive your complete and total healing.

I trust that the information in this book has helped you as much as it has helped me. If you learn what I learned, believe what I believe and do what I did, then you will receive what I received!

Praise God, for *I am HEALED!*

21

A Prayer for Health and Healing

Father, in the mighty Name of Jesus, I confess Your Word concerning health and healing. As I do, I believe that Your Word will not return to You void, but will accomplish exactly what it says it will.

I believe that I am healed according to I Peter 2:24. Your Word says that Jesus Himself took my infirmities and bore my sicknesses (Mat. 8:17). Therefore, I boldly stand with great confidence on the authority of Your Word. I declare that I am redeemed from the curse of sickness and I refuse to tolerate its symptoms.

Satan, I speak to you in the Name of Jesus and I proclaim that your principalities, powers, rulers of the darkness of this world, and spiritual wickedness in heavenly places are bound from operating against me in any way. I am loosed from out of your hand. I am the property of Almighty God and I give you no place in me. I dwell in the secret place of the Most High God and I abide under the shadow of the Almighty, whose power no enemy can withstand.

Now Father, I believe Your Word that says, "The angel of the Lord encamps round about me and delivers me from every evil work. No evil shall befall me, no plague or calamity shall come near my dwelling."

I confess that Your Word abides in me and that it is life and medicine to my flesh. The law of the Spirit of life in Christ Jesus operates in me, and I am free from the law of sin and death.

I hold fast to my confession of Your Word and I stand immovable, knowing that health and healing belong to me *NOW,* in the Name of Jesus, Amen.

Now, begin consistently using your shield of faith, by praising and thanking God for your healing. And if at any time you should see or feel any manifestation of the illness, use your shield.

Prayer To Make Jesus the Lord of Your Life
For Salvation (How to become a Christian)

Heavenly Father, in the Name of Jesus, I present myself to You. I pray and ask you to forgive my sins and ask Jesus to be Lord over my life. According to Romans 10:9, I believe it in my heart, so I say it with my mouth: Jesus has been raised from the dead. This moment I make Him the Lord over my life.

Jesus come into my heart. I believe this moment that I am saved. I say it now: I am reborn. I am a Christian. I am a child of Almighty God.

Amen.

Prayer For Baptism in the Holy Spirit
(How to receive the baptism in the Holy Spirit)

Heavenly Father, I am a believer. I am Your child and You are my Father. Jesus is my Lord. I believe with all my heart that Your Word is true.

Your Word says that if I ask, I will receive the Holy Spirit, so in the Name of Jesus Christ, my Lord, I am asking You to fill me to overflowing with Your precious Holy Spirit.

Jesus, baptize me in the Holy Spirit. Because of Your Word, I believe that I now receive and I thank You for it. By faith, I believe that the Holy Spirit is within me.

Now, Holy Spirit, rise up within me as I praise my God. I fully expect to speak with other tongues as You give me the utterance.

Amen.